God's
Missionary

OTHER DOHNAVUR BOOKS

— — — — — — — — —

May we also suggest:
A Chance to Die
A Biography of Amy Carmichael
by Elisabeth Elliot Gren
published by
Baker Book House

Amy Carmichael

God's Missionary

with a foreword by

Elisabeth Elliot

CLC ❖ PUBLICATIONS
Fort Washington, Pennsylvania 19034

Published by CLC ❖ Publications

U.S.A.
P.O. Box 1449, Fort Washington, PA 19034

GREAT BRITAIN
51 The Dean, Alresford, Hants. SO24 9BJ

AUSTRALIA
P.O. Box 419M, Manunda, QLD 4879

NEW ZEALAND
10 MacArthur Street, Feilding

ISBN 0-87508-323-4

Printed in the United States of America

NOTE TO FIRST EDITION

The vows of God are on me, and I may not stay
To play with shadows, or pluck earthly flowers
Till I my work have done, and rendered up account.

While this manuscript was being written, and afterwards before it was sent to the printer, a little group of missionaries waited upon God about it, and one of them prayed: "Lord, we know that it will go to those who have left home and all for Thy sake. If it must wound—bathe it in tenderness, Lord."

With this prayer we send it out: "If it must wound—would that it need not—but if it must—*bathe it in tenderness, Lord!*"

Here are its three basic themes:

DISENTANGLED
"No soldier on service entangleth himself with the affairs of this life; that he may please Him who hath enrolled him as a soldier."—2 Tim. 2:4, R.V.

SEPARATED
"When either man or woman shall make a special vow, the vow of a Nazirite, to

separate himself unto the Lord: he shall separate himself from wine and strong drink; he shall drink no vinegar of wine, or vinegar of strong drink, neither shall he drink any liquor of grapes, nor eat fresh grapes or dried. All the days of his separation shall he eat nothing that is made of the grapevine, from the kernels even to the husk."—Num. 6:2–4, R.V.

CROWNED

"Neither shall he go out of the sanctuary, . . . for the crown of the anointing oil of his God is upon him."—Lev. 21:12.

NOTE TO THIRD REPRINT

It is a surprise that such a book has been wanted again. If criticism, fair and perhaps sometimes otherwise, could have killed it, it would have been dead long ago. Its fortunes have been varied. It has been tossed into the fire, flung across bungalows, torn into fragments and thrown into wastepaper baskets, dissected, misquoted, written against in "opposition tracts," used as a foil for opposite thought in at least one missionary training-college, and sometimes all but smothered by too appreciative affection. And yet it refuses to die. As it goes out again, it goes with prayer for forgiveness for anything amiss in it, and with longing that it may help some young soul (it was not written for old souls) a little nearer its goal. "To which end we also pray for you that our God may count you worthy of His calling and· fulfill every desire of goodness, and every good work of faith with power."

NOTE TO FIFTH REPRINT

This little book has gone out very quietly; and now very quietly it goes out again. May the Lord, at whose feet every page was laid as it was first written, carry it whithersoever He will.

Amy Carmichael
Dohnavur Fellowship

O PRINCE OF GLORY

O Prince of Glory, who dost bring
   Thy sons to glory through Thy Cross,
Let me not shrink from suffering,
   Reproach, or loss.

The dust of words would smother me;
   Be all to me anathema
That turns me from Gethsemane,
   And Golgotha.

If Thy dear Home be fuller, Lord,
   For that a little emptier
My house on earth, what rich reward
   That guerdon were.

And by the borders of my day
   The river of Thy pleasure flows,
The flowers that blossom by the way
   Who loves Thee knows.

CONTENTS

FOREWORD

Elisabeth Elliot

With the exception of my parents, there is no one who has more deeply influenced my spiritual life than Amy Carmichael, to whose writings I was introduced when I was fourteen years old.

What was it, I have wondered, that so powerfully drew a teenage girl? I think it was the message of the Cross. Amy Carmichael, known to those who loved and worked with her as Amma (an Indian term of respect which can also mean "mother"), was a true soldier of the Cross. I wanted to follow.

As long as I can remember, I hoped the Lord would grant me the privilege of being a foreign missionary. My parents were missionaries when I was born, and we were given missionary books by the dozen. Many well-known missionaries were guests in our home, where we heard their stories firsthand and were inspired.

This little book seemed to set an utterly impossible standard. It was, however, the same standard I found in the words of Jesus: *IF you want to be my disciple, you must give up your right to yourself, take up the Cross, and follow.* What does that mean in practical terms? How can we deny ourselves in a world where from all sides we are being encouraged to love ourselves, do our own thing, let no one jam their morality down our throats? Self-denial was certainly not easy in Jesus' day. It is not easy today. But the simple invitation is open. Jesus speaks to us with matchless love and perfect understanding of the obstacles: *Do you want to be my disciple?*

Any who earnestly answer *yes* will find themselves sobered and challenged by a follower of Christ who speaks with deepest compassion and understanding. She asks questions which are hard to evade. If we take those piercing questions to the foot of the Cross, we will be shown the answers and what we are meant to do about them. God has never issued a command which He will not enable us to obey. Jesus said, "Whoever has my commands and obeys them, he is the one who loves me. He who loves me will be loved by my Father, and I too will love him and show myself to him" (John 14:21).

Amma ends the book with a prayer: *Love is the answer to all things: love ends all questions. Lord, ever more give us this love.*

GOD'S MISSIONARY

We beseech Thee, O Lord, to renew Thy people inwardly and outwardly, that as Thou wouldest not have them to be hindered by bodily pleasures, Thou mayest make them vigorous with spiritual purpose; and refresh them in such sort by things transitory, that Thou mayest grant them rather to cleave to things eternal, through Jesus Christ our Lord.

— Leonine, A.D. 440

1

CROOKED PATTERNS

It was convention week in a hill station in India. The afternoon meeting was just over. A few Christian station-people, some English-speaking Indian friends and the sixty or seventy missionaries who had been listening to the Bible reading were hurrying out to get a cup of tea before the evening meeting. An Indian lady lingered in the empty hall, and the writer, seeing her alone and thinking perhaps she had no friend at hand and might be feeling lonely, sat down beside her. Conversation turned to the Bible reading. The Indian lady's face darkened and she said bitterly, "What is the use of such meetings? You missionaries say one thing and do another!" It was easy to see she had been wounded and soured, but not knowing her history, I could only urge that the meetings were held just because we *recognized* our need of being better than we were.

But this did not satisfy her, and in quick, eager sentences she began to explain herself. She said that her people had noticed that when a missionary first came out, he was usually warm and loving and keen to win souls. Then gradually, she said, it was noticed that he cooled. "And who can say," she concluded, with an intensity that went through her hearer, ". . .who can say you missionaries lead specially holy lives? We Indian Christians observe. We observe you not only when you are at work but when you are off work too. Is there anything remarkable about you? Are you burning-hot people? We look to you to show us patterns *and you are showing us crooked patterns.*"

The words scorched. Discount what we may because of some inward hurt or warp; and granted, thank God, that the picture painted thus is not wholly true, there was enough truth left to lay at least the one who listened low down in the dust.

This writing is not meant for old, experienced missionaries who long ago have made up their minds concerning the questions discussed. It is only meant as a little word offered in all humility to younger fellow-missionaries who have not made up their minds. Comrades in this solemn fight—this awful conflict with awful powers—let us settle it as something that cannot be shaken: We are here to live holy, loving, lowly lives. We cannot do this unless we walk very, very close to our Lord Jesus. Anything that would hinder us from the closest walk that is possible to us till we see Him face to face is not for us. We need to be sensitive to the first approach of the hindering thing. For the sake of the souls that may be stumbled if we turn even ever so little aside, for the sake of our Master's glory—dearer surely to us than all else—let us ask Him now to show us whether in anywise we have been showing "crooked patterns."

If this message should reach a new recruit, one would say the same word, only turning it a little: Will you not wait upon your Lord before you come out, and every day thereafter from the first hour on board ship onwards, asking Him to keep *you*, as we ask Him now to keep *us*, from showing "crooked patterns"?

2

FACTS WHICH
COMPELLED THIS WRITING

Some years ago three missionaries in India, in three different mission stations, were, unknown to each other, seeking light upon the question of separation to God for service.

They had been trained in various schools of thought, but each had learned that to show out the life of our Lord Jesus, and to be a soul-winner, one must live close to the Master, and each came to the mission field longing to win souls.

But they felt themselves befogged, for the traditions of the stations to which they had been appointed did not lean towards separation to the Lord and to His work as they, at least, understood it. There were things crowded into the life for which there had been no room before; there were things crowded out for which much room had been made in the days of earnest preparation for this very service—and they were bewildered and distressed, fearing on the one hand lest they should be lacking in humility if they withstood the influences brought to bear upon them by those whom they sincerely respected, and fearing on the other hand lest they should lose touch with their Lord if they did not so withstand.

Of the three, two gradually gave in, but they lost ground, and went on losing ground, till, startled at finding how much they had lost, they went back to the point from which they had started—the position they had been taught to take at home—of simple untrammeled separation unto God.

Afterwards, in speaking of it, one of them said: "If only I had been warned before I came out! But I knew nothing whatever about it. Why was I never told?"

Perhaps she *had* been told, but not in plain language. Perhaps she did not understand that all over the mission field the sent reflect the senders. Is the Church at home one upon this matter?

The third stood strong, but she found it hard, and in telling us about it she said much as the other had said: "If only I had been prepared! Could not something be written to give new recruits an idea of what they may have to go through when first they come out?" To the objection that to do so would involve a sort of "telling out of school," which is of all things most against the grain, she answered: "Perhaps one ought to be willing even for that *for the sake of souls.*"

A young clergyman, straight from home, stood on the veranda of a mission bunga-low and talked with one who had just come down from the up-country station to which he was bound. Later on he spoke of what he had heard: "I wish I had made up my mind," he said, "but, the fact is, I never realized the thing would meet me out here." And he told us how Society had been a snare to him at home. "But I thought I had done with it when I became a missionary."

He had not done with it. He went off to his station without making up his mind as to what course he should pursue. He found the stream too strong for him; he was wrecked on the rock of compromise; he is at home today.

But what of some who are not at home today but whose influence could not be described as spiritual? What of those who are hindrances to the deeper life in the mission house rather than helps?

Remembering these things, we are writing.

We are writing to "ourselves" from the

standpoint of one who has come to the East for the sake of the people of the East. We do not touch upon any other phase of life, or any other branch of service, and we take it that when we find ourselves among our countrymen the rule also holds good:

We are to know *nothing* among any save Jesus Christ, and Him crucified.

For our calling, by its very nature, calls us apart from everything else; it has for its object nothing less than this: the showing of Christ, the living of Christ, among those who do not know Him. The love of our God must shine through us unhindered if we would live to Him here. Surely, whatever makes for holiness of life, for the clearing of the glass through which the light shines, *this is for us and nothing else.*

So—is not our calling a *special* calling? The world so regards it. We are supposed to have understood this and accepted it at the beginning of our lives as missionaries. "We have good hope that you have well weighed and pondered these things with yourselves long before this time, and that you have clearly determined by God's grace *to give yourselves wholly to this office* whereunto it hath pleased God to call you: so that, as much as lieth in you, you will apply yourselves wholly to this one thing, and draw all your cares and studies this way."

This applies, of course, to the missionary's life on board ship as much as to his life on shore. Take St. Paul as our example. He stood forth in the midst of his shipmates and said, "God, whose I am, and whom I serve, . . ." Can we imagine him frittering away his time in aimless trifles, matters which had not as their end the salvation of the people on board or his own preparation for the battle before him? Could our attitude of life on board ship be always described in that single sentence: *"God, whose I am, and whom I serve"*?

3

ENTANGLEMENTS

What is the ideal of God's missionary? He is to be a Soldier, disentangled; a Nazirite, separated; a Priest, crowned. God's missionary is a Soldier on service out on campaign, and he cannot be entangled in the affairs of this life, "the little affairs," as the Greek has it. They are so little as compared with the great affairs of the War. Does not the word "disentangled" run straight across much that is sometimes accepted as admissible and even desirable in the Lord's soldier?

There is the *social* entanglement: such and such things are expected of us, and we cannot do what is required in this direction and at the same time get the quiet we know we must secure if we are to go on in strength and in calmness of spirit. There are afternoon functions which, to a conscientious worker, may often involve a crush somewhere else if the countless things that do not show when they are done (but are missed if they are not done) are to be peacefully accomplished. There are the late hours, simple enough for those whose duties do not call them up at dawn; but for those who, to have any sort of undisturbed quiet, must not only be up by dawn but awake the dawn, quite another matter. "It was so late when I got home that I was too tired to read or have proper quiet time," said one in speaking of these social duties, so-called. Quiet time—the word is vital.

This little book was about to go out for the fourth time when a girl who had read it at home said, "There is nothing in it about modern women's dress, and nothing about useless talk." It is true there is not and, to be frank, it is not easy to write about either; thorns and briars lie round about these subjects:

Dress:

> Dead to the world and its applause
> To all the customs, fashions, laws,
> Of those who hate the humbling Cross.

Are the words too old to matter now? I cannot think so. But let us go to our Lord, the Crucified, and ask Him what He thinks about it. And if He asks us to change our ways even in this, for His sake and for the sake of those whom we might help if we cared more for Him, and our windows were open towards Jerusalem and not towards any earthly city, shall we not do it?

And *talk*: We should write it down as a law of the house that those who are absent are to be not to be discussed to their detriment, that no belittling stories are told of anyone, nor anything said about anyone unless it passes through the three sieves: Is it true? kind? necessary? We must humble ourselves lest ever, unawares, we break this law. There is an astonishing amount of talk of the kind that can harm the spirit of those whom we are discussing. The frothy talk of nothingness, the mere noise of words that can dull and make dusty a whole table of Christian people, will not taste good to us if by God's grace we hold to that law. Talk can pull down as well as build up, and it can entrap and weaken in a very curious way. But the talk that is the kind Christ would enjoy—frank and simple and sincere and happy as the song of the birds— this kind of talk lifts up and helps. Imagination is appropriate here. Imagine the Lord at table or in the room (*and He is*): How would our talk sound to Him? All we need, all we want, is to have His ungrieved Presence with us always.

And there is the entanglement of *overwork*. Who has not known it? The more we love our work, the keener we are to do it well; the more the burden of souls unreached weighs upon our hearts, the greater our joy in reaching them. How very subtle the form this entangling peril takes, and we are most likely to slip into it before we are aware.

And there is another. I would not touch upon it were it not that it is so terribly familiar, so deadly in its entangling: the unconfessed, perhaps unrealized, awakening of *ambition*, the love of the praise of man that bringeth a snare.

Suddenly, to us thus entangled, comes a call for the exercise of special spiritual energy. Someone has to be dealt with in some definite way. A trial, from which the flesh shrinks back dismayed, waits for us around the next corner. There is a sense of coming conflict; we feel the air thick with contending forces—good and evil—and the evil so terribly strong. Oh, those bonds—invisible cords—why do they hold one so? "As a thread of tow is broken when it toucheth the fire"—we think of that, and call upon the God of fire to burn the bonds and set us free to fight this fight for that soul, to enable us to stand ourselves peaceful and strong in heavenly places in Christ Jesus. But is it that the Lord is farther from us than He used to be? For we fail. And thus—and who that has gone through it can ever forget it?—is there not a grief too grievous to be borne, as the very heart breaks with the shame and the sorrow of the thought: *If I had spent more time with God for souls I should have had more power with souls for God*, and been more calm myself in this turmoil of great waters? For the powers of darkness are as strong as ever they were. Times have not changed since the days of St. Paul. The fight with the spirits of evil is just as desperate now as it was then. The stern condition still holds good: "This kind goeth not out but by prayer and fasting." *We cannot go in for entanglements of any sort and expect spiritual power at the same time.*

"The evangelization of the heathen world"—it is Coillard of the Zambezi who said it—"is a desperate struggle with the Prince of Darkness, and with everything his rage can stir up in the shape of obstacles, vexations, oppositions and hatred, whether by circumstances or by the hand of man. *It is a serious task. It should mean a life of consecration and faith.*"

It is not for nothing that the soldier's word "entanglement" is used only once again in the New Testament, and then in connection with something dangerous. It is used of those who, having escaped "the miasmas of the world," are drawn back into them and "overcome."

We dread malarial fever, and fear lest it should get hold of us and drive us out of the mission field. Should we less dread this spiritual malaria, the fever of a restless soul, which has a power, we know not how, to enervate the very fiber of our being and so unnerve us for the fight? Surely this is the most dangerous form of fever possible. A fit soul in an unfit body is doubtless uncomfortably crippled, but it is not wholly ineffective; but what is the good of a fit body with an unfit soul inside it? It may as well go home at once for all the fighting it will do on the mission battlefield.

But is there not a better way?

> *Searcher of spirits,*
> *Try Thou my reins and heart.*
> *Cleanse Thou my inward part,*
> *Turn, overturn and turn.*
> *Wood, hay and stubble see,*
> *Spread out before Thee,*
> *Burn, burn.*

> *Savior of sinners,*
> *Out of the depths I cry,*
> *Perfect me or I die:*
> *Perfect me, patient One;*

In Thy revealing light,
I stand confessed outright,
Undone.

O to be holy!
Thou wilt not say me nay
Who movest me to pray.
Enable to endure:
Spiritual cleansing Fire,
Fulfill my heart's desire.
Make pure.

4

FROM THE KERNELS
EVEN TO THE HUSK

God's true missionary is a Nazirite, who has "made a special vow, the vow of one separated, to separate himself unto the Lord."

This "special vow" meant total abstinence from certain things which were not wrong in themselves and which, to others, might be beneficial. "All the days of his separation shall he eat nothing that is made of the grapevine, from the kernels even to the husk."

Do we never, as missionaries, hear the question "What is the harm of it?" asked about reading certain books, following certain pursuits, taking our recreation in certain ways?

Perhaps we have been hard at the language, and need change of thought and rest of brain. "What is the harm of the latest novel, even if it happens to be rather unprofitable?" And we (who have not time to read one out of a thousand of the real books that have been written) spend a precious hour by deliberate choice over something not worthwhile; and when our immediate world interrupts us, breaking in upon us with some call, do we find that we come back to it with quite undistracted gladness? Or do we feel that we have, as it were, to try to come back from somewhere and pull ourselves together, and gird up the loins of our mind, before we are ready to throw ourselves heart and soul into the thick of the fight again?

Then, to rise higher on the scale of desire, in a land where, on every side, almost unexplored regions lie waiting for the coming of the pioneer—ancient literature, the history of nations, of religions, strange tribes, customs, folklore, languages—there is a fascination and a "draw" which appeal strongly to a mind with a bent towards research. Up to a certain point—and no one can draw the line for another—such knowledge is power. But beyond it——?

Let Dr. Roberts, of Tientsin, speak. He recognized it as his clear duty to give necessary time to the consideration of every case, so that he might do the best possible for each patient. "But then," he said, "I might easily go a step beyond that, and yield to the temptation that comes to

me as a professional man to study closely
cases rarely seen in England, with a view
to special proficiency. If, to do this, I must
neglect Chinese study and spiritual work
in the wards, life is not long enough for
everything." So he preferred to fill up his
time with work which seemed most likely
to hasten the coming of his Master's Kingdom, laying these possibilities of greater
professional efficiency at the Lord's feet
as freewill offerings of love. He said he
thought all Christians felt at times a longing to let others see that the followers of
Jesus could successfully compete with
others in various spheres of work. There
was nothing absolutely wrong in this desire; yet he thought, if we were only willing to give up for the Lord's sake possibilities of success in other fields than
those which tended directly to the ad-
vancement of His Kingdom, He would give
us a very real sense of His approval and
acceptance of such freewill offerings.

And so he "narrowed down" his life,
bent the whole force of it to what "tended
directly" to soul-winning. But was earth
the poorer to him, and is Heaven the emptier to him, because he did so?

In Bishop Paget's *Spirit of Discipline* he
speaks of lives which, by their clearness
and freedom, their successful resolution

not to be brought under the power of things which domineer over most men, arrest the attention of those who look on. The men and women who so lived were born and nurtured, as that powerful paragraph puts it, in conditions like our own, and yet they were "so splendidly unhindered by the things which keep us back." We think of such and are ashamed. How far, how very far we are from any such great living!

What was their secret? Is it not worthwhile to find it out? Some of them have told it to us:

I do not think there is anything so essential to real service for God . . . as an entire separation and devotion to the work. Thus speaks Arnot of Central Africa; thus speaks every man and woman whose life has made more than a passing flicker in the spiritual realm. Whether among our fellow-countrymen or the people of the land, it is the life that has no time for trifling that tells.

We all long to live to the uttermost,

> Not with the crowd to be spent,
> Not without aim to go round
> In an eddy of purposeless dust,
> Effort unmeaning and vain,

in very truth to live, to touch souls to eternal issues. Is there no less straightly marked path to reach that goal? *There is not.* But is not this strange talk for the Lord's own lovers? Ours should be the love that asks not "How little?" but "How much?"; the love that pours out its all and revels in the joy of having anything to pour on the feet of its Beloved; love that laughs at limits—rather, does not see them, would not heed them if it did. How such talk as that feeble, futile "What is the harm?" falls from us and is forgotten when we see Calvary, the Crucified, the risen-again Rabboni of our souls!

Who that one moment has the least descried Him,
Dimly and faintly, hidden and afar,
Doth not despise all excellence beside Him,
Pleasures and powers that are not and that are—

Ay amid all men bear himself thereafter
Smit with a solemn and a sweet surprise,
Dumb to their scorn and turning on their laughter
Only the dominance of earnest eyes?

5

SURELY THERE IS NO HARM IN RAISINS?

"Surely there is no harm in recreation?" This is a question we have heard asked in tones of reproach, surprise, or even disgust, depending upon the frame of mind of the questioner.

To this question we answer, "No, if by recreation is meant *re-equipment for future work with no leakage of spiritual power*." We must have a fresh influx of life for both soul and body, or we shall dry up and become deserts in a desert. But where are our fresh springs to be? That is the main question. "All my fresh springs are in Thee." Can we say so truthfully? Or is it not a fact that—with some of us at least—certain forms of recreation have, perhaps quite insensibly to us, got out of their place, and hinder, rather than help, all-round robustness of life?

And here we must remind ourselves again that we are writing *to ourselves*. We are not dealing with the question of the rightness or wrongness of this and that for others, but whether we, as God's missionaries, have not something to learn from the Nazirite's special vow, and how it bore upon harmless indulgence in harmless things. The essence of that vow was abstention from things which were lawful in themselves but not expedient for him. Even raisins were contraband. Surely there is no harm in raisins?

In the *Student Movement* of March 1900 there is an article on "Prayer and Fasting." We quote from the last paragraph. The speaker has just referred to the discovery of the papyrus in Egypt upon which were inscribed a few of the supposed "Sayings of Jesus," one of which was this: "Unless ye fast from the world ye shall not find the Kingdom of Heaven."

"It is not a difficult idea to follow, and it takes you to the very heart of the thought of Jesus. It is for you as missionaries, and it is just as much for us who are trying to serve our Lord at home, to treat the world not only in its corruptions but in its legitimate joys, in all its privileges and blessings, as a subject that we should touch at a distance, and with strict reserve and abstinence, feeling that if we are caught by its spirit or fed upon its meat, we shall not feel the breath of the

Highest nor receive the manna that falleth from Heaven. Therefore we are bound to look upon the world, with all its delights and all its attractions, with suspicion and with reserve. *It is not for us, not for us.* We are called into a higher Kingdom, we are touched with a diviner Spirit. It is not that He *forbids* us this or that indulgence or comfort of our life; it is not that He is *stern*, making upon us the call of the ascetic: but it is that we who love our Lord, and we whose affections are set on the things that are in Heaven, *voluntarily and gladly lay aside* the things that charm and ravish the world, that, for our part, our hearts may be ravished with the things of Heaven, and that our whole being may be poured forth in constant and unreserved devotion in the service of the Lord who died to save us."

"A pure heart," says Tauler, "is one to which all that is *not of God* is strange and jarring."

If the first question a missionary asks about a hill station concerns the amusements there; if more important things are crowded out by a tournament of some sort, or a whirl of picnics, or a game of bridge; if private theatricals are the order of the day "because they are better than gossip" (but why gossip at all?); if a word spoken upon the subject of excessive devotion to recreation is bitterly resented; if this booklet, not only because of the way it touches the subject but because it touches it at all, calls down a storm of criticism—if these things be so, we say, "Comrades in the war of God, has not something got out of its place? Is it not time we called a halt and searched ourselves in the searchlight of the Cross?"

6

FIRST THINGS FIRST

G ranted that we all need exercise, could we not take it more than we do with the people for whom we are here? Could we not make *them* more our friends and find recreation in being with *them*?

Many a Christian worker on a college campus has found games with his students not less invigorating than the perhaps-more-perfectly-arranged game elsewhere. Some have proved that the exercise taken in the walk to the village for the evening preaching has been none the less recreative because we had the Lord for our Companion and were out on His business; and we have found it true that, while we communed together, Jesus Himself drew near and went with us, and made our hearts burn within us while He talked with us by the way. What better recreation than the re-creating of the holy fire? The glow of it makes one strong!

Or, if rest rather than exercise is the need of the hour, there are those who have found it close at hand; or, rather, it has found them as they "let the elastic go." Trench, in his *Synonyms of the New Testament,* tells us that the word used in 2 Thessalonians 1:7 and translated "rest" means the relaxing or letting down of cords or strings which have before been strained or drawn tight. Perhaps we need to know more of this perfectly simple form of rest, the "letting go" of the strained strings—the relaxation of the tension.

And this, in the writer's experience, is greatly helped by a book which carries the mind far away from the life which presses all around. God's blessing on those who send such books! For, after all, the mind needs change of air as much as does the body. One of the secrets of going on is to get away. This may sound like crossing out a sentence on a previous page; it does not do so. All depends upon where you go when you get away. Breathe tainted air or air that is merely relaxing, and you come back no better. Breathe sea air or mountain air or any kind of air that is pure and strong, and you come back refreshed.

Then, as regards being with our Indian friends not only in work hours but in play, such a life tends to make us become more and more one with them, and we have opportunities of helping them which are unknown to those whose recreation is taken entirely, or as much as may be, apart from them. So, even if it should mean something of *sacrifice*, is it not worth a sacrifice? And one of the best results is that we are on the spot *if we are needed.* Suppose that by being away out of reach—for the time being at least—we missed a chance to win a soul for Christ or help one to draw nearer to Him? Would an eternity of recreation with congenial friends make up to us for that one loss?

But some will smile at all this as feeble and foolish, and some will say, "Very unpractical." We can only say, "*It works.*" There are men and women on the mission fields today who began by going in for the usual round there because they were told they must. But they are just as strong and well now that they have given all up in favor of a life lived *with* the people and *for* them! They can witness gladly to the bond that binds them to their Indian brothers and sisters—a link all the closer, surely, because *they* come first in real love, and because *they* know they do. *We can never know an Eastern people*—it is fallacious to imagine we do—*while we find our chief recreation to be an escape from their companionship into the society of our fellow-Europeans.* The people of the land are keenly observant: they mark our preferences in the choice of our friends, as in everything else. If we find our rest and pleasure in being away from them, will they open out to us and let us understand them? No, we shall be farther away from them than we know, and however affectionate they are, there will always be a certain reserve in their confidence—unrecognized by us, perhaps, because we are not near enough to them to know that it exists.

Do not misunderstand. The thought of these paragraphs is not to lay down a hard-and-fast rule for which bondage would be a fitting name. It is rather to suggest that to be recreative, recreation need not draw us away from our people. Sometimes it will, but need it be so always?

The tendency of English society to keep us apart has been noted again and again by missionaries in every land. Bishop Steere of Africa writes with force that the company of Europeans keeps a man separate from the people of the land and that no one will ever be a good missionary who cannot be happy among them. And Ragland, of India, urges the new recruit to cultivate close contact with the Hindu mind lest he lose his first missionary aspirations and begin to prefer European society and work, and to look wistfully towards home.

A plea urged on behalf of such forms of recreation as take us away from our people not only in the flesh but in the spirit is that "unless we get some variety, we grow rutty, groovy, morbid, liverish, unsociable, narrow-minded." And so, for the sake of our own character and mental development, we "really must indulge in a little harmless 'dissipation' occasionally." But does this answer to the facts?

Does such a withdrawing tend to make us gentler under the stress of the contradictions of sinners, more able in quietness to bear up under their burden and their strife? Does it make the work for which we are here more precious? Does it help us to see more to love in the people and less to criticize? If these good things or any of them are wrought in us by that which we call "harmless dissipation" (but try to think of the word in association with Calvary, and it withers before it shapes), then let us continue as we are. But if it be not so, shall we not have done with it?

We are variously made. What rests one person wearies another. The great thing is to find what rests *us* most, what sends *us* back to our work most truly strengthened and refreshed in body, soul and spirit. Our thought here, as all through this booklet, is not to define another's duty but to urge that each of us should be sincere in finding out our own. Let us be honest in the determination that we will not sacrifice the *spiritual* to anything whatever! Recreation for our threefold being *is* possible. He who knoweth our frame, and remembereth that we are dust, has wonderful ways of leading us in this matter, if only we are single-hearted enough to be led; and there is a sense, even physically, in which the Joy of the Lord is strength.

Comrades, "First things first." We all say it. Let us do it. And the *first thing* first of all. What is the missionary's first thing? Let a missionary speak: "Always bearing about in the body the dying of the Lord Jesus, that the life also of Jesus may be manifested in our mortal flesh."

Jesus. Redeemer and my One Inspirer,
Heat in my coldness, set my life aglow;
Break down my barriers; draw, yea, draw me nigher,
Thee would I know, whom it is life to know.

Deepen me, rid me of the superficial,
From pale delusion set my spirit free;
All my interior being quick unravel;
Pluck forth each thread of insincerity.

Thy vows are on me, O to serve Thee truly—
Love perfectly, in purity obey—
Burn, burn, O Fire; O Wind, now winnow throughly;
O Sword, awake against the flesh and slay.

O that in me
  Thou, my Lord, may see
    Of the travail of Thy soul,
      And be satisfied.

7

THE CROSS IS
THE ATTRACTION

Separation unto God in its true sense does not mean narrowness. St. Paul seemed to think that being separated should have quite the opposite effect. "You find no narrowness in my love, but the narrowness is in your own" (2 Cor. 6:12, Conybeare and Howson's translation), and in order to get rid of their narrowness he advises the Corinthian Christians to come out and be separate—to come out from the unclean ways of the world.

He strikes another note as well: "Where the Spirit of the Lord is, there is liberty." Liberty for what? Liberty to reflect as in a mirror the glory of the Lord. Here is the positive corollary to the "negativeness" of separation.

"But to win the world we must meet it halfway," some may object. Must we? Who says so?

How can we missionaries most effectively touch our world for Christ?

It is possible, we must realize, to "touch" the spirit of the world at many points with the best intentions and yet make no appreciable difference in its worldliness. We may influence the tone of a community for the space of the hour we spend in it, but does our presence there lead to opportunities for direct, unequivocal work for our Lord? And if not, is our "touching it" worthwhile?

"But there is no 'world' in that sense now. The word has gone out of fashion." Possibly; and with it certain tremendous words in the New Testament. (We know this is vain talk, a veneer that deceives no one.) The "world" *is*, and in many an open port in the East, and in many a city and country station too, *a line has to be drawn*, however unwillingly. The nebulous simply cannot be.

Sometimes the question hardly rises. There are civilians who serve India in Christ's name, and where *they* are there is no question of joining forces or crossing gulfs. We and they are *one* force, and there need be no gulf. What we are considering now is the far more difficult position—where alongside us is a life in which there is no room for the Lord Jesus Christ. And yet those who live that way need Him as much as any. Can we reach them by being as like them as possible (only, per-haps, a little more decorously dull)? Is that the line of power? We hold that it is *not*. How then are these hardened ones to be won?

The Cross is the attraction. What if this short, forceful sentence contains the an-swer to the question that rises in the heart as, convinced of the futility of one way of approach, it seeks another, a more direct one? Over and over again it has been proved that to those who will go straight on, unswerved by any argument or in-ducement to turn aside to more round-about ways of access, *opportunities no strategy or plan could have created* are most freely and wonderfully given. Our only responsibility is not to miss them as they pass. To speak for our Lord, then, is not to write on sand. Blessed be the Lord our Strength, *strong* to allure, *mighty* to save, who uses the very Cross of shame to attract the wandering souls of men!

8

THE TWO CROWNS

We have come to the last thought: God's true missionary is an anointed Priest. And as the result of his consecration, he is crowned: "For the crown of the anointing oil of his God is upon him" (Lev. 21:12). He does not want to win the crown of earthly glory or of worldly popularity or of literary fame. The crown of his God is enough for him. He may not leave the Presence-chamber. He does not *want* to leave it. "Am *I* not enough for thee, Mine own?" He has heard the voice and answered, "Thou forever and alone art enough for me."

And the end of it all? Does not our heart burn as we look beyond, unto the reward? "For what is our hope, or joy, or crown of rejoicing; are not even ye in the presence of our Lord Jesus Christ at His coming?" For *ye*—these whom we love better than life, very soul of our soul—*ye* are our glory and joy! Even as one writes these words, borne along by a great wave of glorious gladness because of them, a thought comes about the two crowns: the crown of the anointing, the crown of the rejoicing—they are made, as it were, of the same piece of gold. For if we, even we—less than the least though we be—do by this grace receive the anointing of our God; and if, constrained by that solemn anointing, we stay with Him and do "not go out"—then by His wonderful, infinite love we shall be crowned with that other crown, the crown of converts won for Him, when we stand in the presence of our Lord Jesus Christ, to go out no more forever!

Crowned with crowns to lay at His feet, He who was crowned with thorns for us— is not the joy of the thought of it enough to set us singing as God's birds sing—for very bliss of being? Think of the joy that is set before us—joy after joy in endless perspective—joy after joy!

Here, then, is the way through the fog, straight and clear and all lit up:

> *Christ the Son of God hath sent me*
> *Through the midnight lands;*
> *Mine the mighty ordination*
> *Of the piercèd Hands.*

We stop and read what we have written,

and we feel, more than even its critics can, how very inadequate it is, how crudely expressed, how unconvincing where we most want to convince. We can only let it go, trusting to our Lord to use it if it speaks His truth; trusting that it may steady some waverer somewhere to stand, or win someone who has been drifting downstream to fight up against the current again. Or—God grant it—help ever so little to save even one from shipwreck on the rock of compromise.

Comrades, let us be resolute. Let us, by whatever name we are called, be Soldiers, Nazirites, Priests. Some will praise us, some will blame us; let us not care too much about either praise or blame. Let us live looking up, looking on, standing true by the grace of Him who has called us.

Perhaps we should best go away somewhere alone with our Lord and ask Him to guide us. We may be perplexed. He will explain. Things may be badly put. He will put them perfectly. We may be distressed about what will happen if we act upon the thoughts that are growing strong within us. He will make all things right if only we follow and obey.

Have we not proved this true before? Shall we not prove it true again?

Some years ago a young girl, while absent from her mission station, waited upon God for guidance about a certain controversial matter. She settled it on the less usual side, and wrote at once to explain her position to her senior missionary. She dreaded returning to her station, and prayed much for courage and humility to take her stand and hold to it bravely and yet in the evident meekness of Jesus. But upon her return she found that God had been working for her, and she wrote joyfully—

> Better hath He been for years
>   Than my fears.

But, however it may be, surely there is nothing to fear. It is inconceivable that our Master would leave us to stand alone when we are standing for Him.

How could He? For He has said, "I will never leave thee nor forsake thee." And the word "forsake" conveys the idea of "leaving comrades exposed to peril in the conflict, or forsaking them in some crisis of danger." He could never do that. Even if He had not told us so, we should have known it. It would not be like our Lord. Do not let us fear to follow the inward leading of Jesus. "If any man serve Me, let him follow Me; and where I am, there shall also My servant be."

9

LOVE IS THE ANSWER TO ALL THINGS

It is possible that all that has been said is wide of the mark where many of us are concerned; we may have few or no temptations regarding what is known as open worldliness of life. But here is the crux: Are we "other-worldly" in the secret center of our soul? Is there no compromise ever there? Does the rush of work never get in between our Master and ourselves? Is there no failure in this direction, or leakage of spiritual strength? Or are we looking at others and what they do—or perhaps at what they expect *us* to do—and are we trying to do this at the expense of time for rest and quiet with our Lord? "Let *Me* see thy countenance; let *Me* hear thy voice," our Lord beseeches. Have not these words, so full of wistful love, come to us sometimes and stopped us in some outward whirl, and bidden us go into inward calm and let *Him* see our countenance and let *Him* hear our voice?

For there are forms of compromise—in the depths of our hearts we know it—that pursue the missionary beyond the outward bounds of worldliness. May God search us, and try us, and show us if we are living on lower levels than He intends for us—living in the shallows when He meant us to dwell deep in the heart of eternal love.

•　　•　　•

Lord, Thou knowest: Thou knowest all things. Thou knowest that I love Thee.

"But, because I am as yet weak in love and imperfect in virtue, therefore do I stand in need of being strengthened and comforted by Thee. Wherefore visit me again and again; and instruct me by all holy discipline.

"Free me from evil passions and heal my heart of all inordinate affections; that, being inwardly healed and thoroughly cleansed, I may become fit to love, strong to suffer, constant to persevere.

"Love is a great thing, a great good indeed, which alone makes light all that is burdensome and bears with even mind all that is uneven. For it carries a burden without being burdened; and it makes all that which is bitter sweet and savory.

"The love of Jesus is noble, and spurs

us to do great things, and excites us to desire always things more perfect.

"Love desires to have its abode above, and not to be kept back by things below.

"Love desires to be at liberty and estranged from all worldly affection, lest its inner view be hindered, lest it suffer itself to be entangled through some temporal interest, or give way through mishap.

"Nothing is sweeter than love; nothing stronger, nothing higher, nothing broader, nothing more pleasant, nothing fuller or better in heaven and in earth; for love is born of God, and can rest only in God above all things created.

"The lover flies, runs, and rejoices; he is free and not held. He gives all for all and has all in all, because he rests in one supreme above all, from whom all good flows and proceeds.

"Love knows no measure, but warmly glows above measure.

"Love feels no burden, regards not labors, would willingly do more than it is able, pleads not impossibility, because it feels sure that it can and may do all things.

"It is able, therefore, to do all things; and it makes good many deficiencies, and frees many things for being carried out, where he who loves not faints and lies down.

"Love watches, and sleeping slumbers not; weary, is not tired; straightened, is not constrained; frightened, is not disturbed; but, like a living flame and a burning torch, it bursts forth upwards and safely over-passes all.

"Whosoever loves knows the cry of this voice."—Thomas à Kempis: *The Imitation of Christ*, Book III, chapter 5.

Love is the answer to all things: love ends all questions. Lord, ever more give us this love.

This book was produced by CLC Publications. We hope it has been helpful to you in living the Christian life. CLC is a literature mission with ministry in over 50 countries worldwide. If you would like to know more about us, or are interested in opportunities to serve with a faith mission, we invite you to write to:

CLC Publications
P.O. Box 1449
Fort Washington, PA 19034